Holding Hands Together

Alan Evans

Grosvenor House
Publishing Limited

This book is published by
Grosvenor House Publishing Ltd
Link House
140 The Broadway, Tolworth, Surrey, KT6 7HT.
www.grosvenorhousepublishing.co.uk

A CIP record for this book
is available from the British Library

Paperback ISBN 978-1-80381-014-0
Hardback ISBN 978-1-80381-013-3

All artwork and photos by Ashley and Katie Evans are copyright
and used by permission.

In Loving Memory of Audrey (Audi) Vera Evans

She was God's gift to me and I to her.
Held close to my heart. Remembered always.

Loved Forever.

Alan Evans-Husband

Children, grandchildren & great-grandchildren
Ashley & Katie
Marcus & Vikki, Jessica & Isabella
Josh & Alexandra, Aria
Nico.

Oliver & Lorraine Quincy, Estelle & Austin

Warren & Juliet Jacob, Nathan & Alex

Milton & Laura Felix, Indie & Ace

Sylvia-Sister

Nephews & Nieces

Simon & Nicola

Andrew & Julia Lucie & Laura

1

THE WORD

You'll never believe it. I've lost a word
I had it yesterday, but now it's gone
I told a friend, He said I was absurd
To lose your voice is bad enough
But to lose a word!
Farcical indeed it is quite unknown
I've searched high searched low
Will I ever find this vital word?
O dear O dear you will not never believe it
It was here yes here all the time
Right under my nose on the tip of my tongue.

Alex (chuck-a-doodles)

by Ashley Evans

2

IT'S GREEN

As I look out of my window
I see twenty shades of green
The grass is green
The trees are green
Green is nature's basic colour
It is comforting on the eye and pleasant to the brain
Science discovered this many years ago
How clever of God to have thought of it first

Lizzie Daley

3

HOLDING HANDS TOGETHER

The day we met was O so good, holding hands together.
Life was such a comfort, holding hands together.
Laughing and crying still holding hands together
In joy and in sadness still holding hands together
With friends short and tall still holding hands together
On land and sea on hill and dale still holding
    hands together
As children came and grew in joy still holding
    hands together
In hard times and good times still holding hands together
Going shopping going to worship still holding
    hands together
In youth in marriage in old age still holding hands together
In illness, pain yet moving forward still holding
    hands together
In sun or rain and even wind and snow still holding
    hands together
Yet soon we had to part as one was called forward
    into Heaven holding hands with Jesus
One left on earth holding hands with Jesus
With Jesus still holding them together hand in hand
With such love wonderful memories together

Juliet

4

PHONE CALL TO MUM

Hello Mum, Happy birthday

Yes Mum it's good to talk

Sorry Mum what did you say?

No Mother the dog is not barking

No Mother I don't have a dog

No Mother I don't have a cat either

Well how are you today?

Yes Mum I am ok no there is no dog here

Mother I do not have a dog

Yes I did have a dog many years ago

Yes his name was Reggy but he died

(continued)

Mum don't get upset he died five years ago

No Mother I don't want another dog

I'm sure your neighbour breeds good dogs

No Mother I do not have a dog

What would you like for your birthday?

No Mother I did not buy you a dog

Pardon Mother, you are glad because you do not like dogs

No I did not send a dog

No Mother I never mentioned dogs you did

No Mother I do not have a dog and it is not barking

Now be at peace I am not sending a dog to you

Look mother what are you going to have for your tea?

Pardon Mother, you are having a what? A hot dog Bye Mum

by Ashley Evans

5

I SEE IT NOW

I see it now
I didn't see it then
For then I saw the attractiveness of a cunning man
One who gave us hope that soon the Romans would be
    defeated
Yes he was big, angry, and he captivated our hopes.
But then disaster, he was captured and imprisoned, chained
Our aspirations lost.
Then new hope arose as the cry rang out
Release unto us Barabbas; Barabbas, Barabbas
Then what shall I do with the King of the Jews
Crucify, Crucify, Crucify away with him
Release unto us Barabbas.
And so it was but...
the hope and joy faded he was no longer attractive
It was this other man – led away to be crucified – nailed to a
    tree.
His look, his face, his words
Forgive them Father for they do not know what they are
    doing.
I could not, will not ever forget that face in agony,
Yet in the mystery of love.
Then I saw, then I felt. Then I knew, see now I see

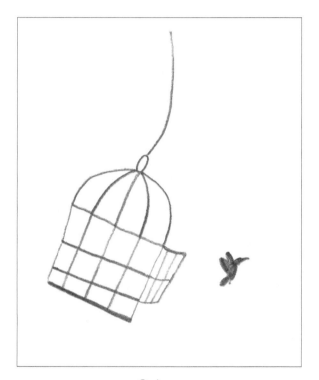

Quincy

6

TRAPPED

I screamed to be free of pressures bending on my head
Why? Is the cry, what difference does it make?
Will my sweated brow and anguished mind
Profit more than prayer contemplating peace?
Which brings more purpose?
The aching back bent in fevered work
Or the song of freedom sung by a gentle bird?
What will be remembered more? The cash I raise
or the tear wiped clean from an anguished face?
Who cares more a working committee or love's
    compassion?

by Ashley Evans

7

FLOW

The azure beauty of the flowing stream
brought joy to my stifled mind.
I watched as it skipped its way jauntily over rounded
    boulders
Its freedom shouting as it made its way along
Finding its passage purposefully round every turn and
    obstacle.
My mind in equal freedom followed the water
as in merriment it passed on by
Trout and Kingfisher caught my eye
as I relaxed on grassy bank so warm and welcoming.
I splashed my feet in its inviting flow.
The ice fresh beck in soothing care
caressed my aching feet in pleasing fashion.
My mind refreshed as I dangled my feet in God's water
and rested in his abiding love.

by Ashley Evans

16

8

THE LITTLE OLD LADY

I woke
Grumpy
And groaning
I was fed up
I set out in a bad frame of mind
I trudged down the street
In the corner of my eye I saw her
A crumpled old lady, in much pain with sticks to help her
Hello I said can I help you
O thank you so much
I was going for a loaf of bread
Brown please
So kind she said
In the shop, your regular order Sir?
No I am shopping for Ida
OK I know Ida, small brown
I paid and left
Thank you Ida said. So good
Her old lined face changed as she gave a great big smile
The smile lit up the street
And also in my mind
Thank you so much you have helped so
No, I said thank you dear Ida
It is you who have helped me.
This grumpy groaning, fed up man found it had all evaporated.

Jessica aged 4

9

THE SPIDER

I watched the spider
He crawled across the floor
Does he know where he is going?
Is he heading for the door?
Has he got a family?
Or is he all alone?
What is he thinking?
He looks all forlorn.
So lonely and alone I have lots of questions to ask him
O dear he has scampered under the settee.

10

SO WHAT IS LIFE?

So what is life?
Is it real or is it just pretence?
Can it be touched or felt or seen?
Is the air I breathe the true oxygen of life
or am I mistaken, in a dream,
What is the true reality of life?

Is it the fumbling of a human form upon
the dust of past hopes and present pain?
Is my strength the only hope for me
can I trust others as they stumble on
from unbelieving imagination to some frustrated cosmic hope?
Can I lift my eyes and nose from the odour of rotted dreams
to see the sunlight of another hope for me?
A hope not wrought by my vain thoughts and feeble strength
but by the sunlight of a power revealed
in the apparent failure of a dying man
A dying that has no stench or foulness of deaths decay
But that from a sweet scent of hope
Transcends the crippled nature of my mind

I may never understand the holy reasoning of the crucified
but in humility I kneel before his love.
With feeble hands I grasp the forgiving nature of his grace

and find myself lifted from the grovelling nature of my stance.
To stand in hope
To see the glory of who he is
and see the true reality of life
and nestle in the bosom of his heart.
He drew me in with compelling power of love
so dynamic, so magnetic, so attractive so….so…
The words are lost upon my lips
but find content within my heart.

I hear his cry –
Go and tell, go share the true reality of life.

by Katie Evans

Lorraine

11

The People Leave

The people leave,
The laughter ceases,
The light goes out
Yet sleep come not
Just the empty thump of nothingness.
The ear-splitting noise of silence,
The stillness of the moving darkness
The buzz of rampant thoughts,
The fear of the unknown path,
A path that transcends the footsteps of man
Where do I go in the labyrinth of sleep?
Will I wake up?
Will the path lead to day?
To light, to people?
Will we laugh again?
What lies in the unknown morrow?
The other side of the barrier of sleep?
If only I could sleep – sleep – sleep ….
Good morning, Sir – tea or coffee?

Alex Daley

12

TEMPEST OF THE MIND

The tempest of the mind
Whirls in vibrating motion,
Hissing its grinding emotion
All is seen as lost.
Then the rescuer of lostness
Whispers his love potion into
the fretting mind – *'Yes,*
My son, I do love you,
You are mine' – these
simple words cascade
In sweet scented colours
Into the troubled bubbling
Waters of my mind and all
Is still, the storm is calm.
'Rest here my child, then
Travel on with me.'

by Ashley Evans

13

Hey Joe

Hey Joe lets go for a walk?
No, I'll just sit here.

Hey Joe lets go to the snooker hall?
No, I'll just sit here.

Hey Joe lets play soccer?
No, I'll just sit here.

Hey Joe lets go for a swim?
No, I'll just sit here.

Hey Joe lets go fishing?
No, I'll just sit here.

Hi Mum
Hi Joe

Hey Joe why are you just sitting?
I have nothing to do.

Jacob

14

Semi Sleep

The NEVER vision of semi sleep
Blurs the words of the book I read.
Was it hope I read or dope?
Was it sin or bin or fin?
Was it right or sight or might?
I cannot tell as sleep begins
To conquer my fuddled thoughts.

Was it – is it – lost it- found it.
Words recede into the haziness of . of .. of …
What was that noise?
With startled nerves I life my head
To see a book lie defeated on the ground
Beside my bed.

Nathan

15

Lord, why is it so hard to pray?

Lord why is it so hard to pray?
After all, it's like talking, isn't it?
Talking to You?
I find it so easy to talk to Joe and Fred,
And Mary and Joan. So what's the difference?
After all You're more interested in me
Than they are; I don't want to be critical but You are.
You are more interested in how I feel
About my wife and my city and my neighbour.
You want to hear from me, You want to listen,
So why don't I talk to You more?

Other people are very interesting when they talk to me
And I listen to them for hours.
Yet You know more, love better, care more fully,
So why don't I listen to You more?

(continued)

You have so much to show me
So *much more* to share with me.
So why, Lord, do I get interested in
So much that is so petty that I fail
To spend much time talking to You,
Listening to you. Why, Lord? What is my problem?
If I have a real problem, why, then Lord, I can talk to You.
I can talk with urgency and passion but when
The problem is solved or gone away, so does
The urgency of prayer and passion evaporate.
Well, here I am again talking about my failure
But thank you, Lord, for listening to me
Perhaps I now ought to be able to be still and listen to you

I love you Lord - **Amen**

by Katie Evans

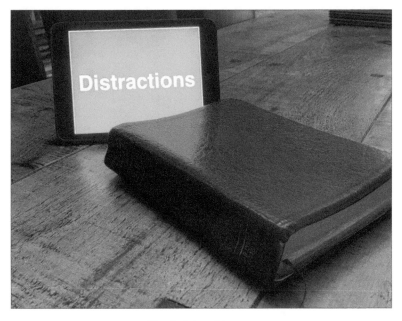

By Ashley Evans

16

The Day

The swirling mist of life is free to breathe
The mystic magic of another day.
It drifts in so sleepily but gathers speed
Until I'm set amidst the frenzy of its grip.
I can, I will, I may, I might, I – I —

The day speeds on, the noise is loud
But its volume is deafened by the quietness of
compelling needs.
The demands are there, they scream
and penetrate the confusion of my mind.
Which shall be first, I cannot tell, I must decide …

I must, I must, the needs demand.
Yet soon the darkness of another night
Sweeps in and there in the hollow of the night
The unmet demands fester in my sleepless mind.

Tomorrow is another day.
The prayers are said, the night progresses on
Toward another day.

17

The Boy So Coy

The boy so coy had joy with toy;
The boy so bright held light with might so tight;
The boy so glum played drum, drank rum, looked dumb;
The boy with cheer dried tear, drank beer so clear;
The boy with eye so dry did spy – a girl!
The boy did marry, her name Carri, his is Barry;
The boy now man, he has a boy
And no money!

Austin

18

I Saw a Word

I saw a word, its's Metastasis.
It sounds so fine, so bright, so Metathesis.
What does it mean?
The question raised, I seek an answer.
Is it bone in foot so grand?
No, you fool, that's Metatasus.
Is it state of equilibrium?
No; don't babble; that's Metastable.
What can it mean, this word that does confound?
Its's transformation of a compound
Into other process of assimilation, I'll be bound,
By an organism that very sound.
Yes. It is, Metastasis!

Estelle

19

Refreshed

The pure air of sweet tranquillity
Descends upon my troubled brow
Like scented mist upon the dew
And evaporates the tension
Of another stressful day.

by Ashley Evans

by Ashley Evans

20

Peace

I lay relaxed in cushioned chair
Enjoying the majesty of silent peace
So goodly energising now for me.
O how wonderful the treasured moment
As the angel of tranquilic harmony
Ushered in from Heaven's portals
mops this fevered brow of mine
And takes my hand enabling me
To face the foe of yet another task.

A task with all its complicated rhythms
Yet made easier by a moment's rest.
A rest not made for idle meanderings
But sweet rest by far that has recharged
The willing hope of action,
and enabled the powerful flow of spirit fed flesh
To tackle and master and complete another job.

by Ashley Evans

21

It Was Good

The beauty of love
The scent of flowers
The sweet sound of rippling streams,
The smile of a child
The gentleness of caring hands
The smell of a new mown meadow after rain
The joy of loving friends
The happiness around a new-born baby
The exhilaration when your team wins
The peace of knowing the risen Saviour.

What a wonderful world
A world in which all men may find peace
And God saw that it was good.

Nico

22

The Grim Face

The grim face of the young man
The fear and anger and hopelessness,
The wickedness in blank eyes
A young body made in the Image of God
Now arched as destruction is strapped to
His body and soul with one intent
To shatter love.
Change the sweet smell of flowers into the stench of death
The sweet sound of a rippling stream to the torrent of hate
The smile of a child into a distorted face of fear
Gentle hands blown apart because you dare to be
Smell of newly mown hay into blood filled abyss of
    destruction.
Caring friend now weeps in hopeless despair,
The new born baby left a crying orphan.
The inner anger a mindless destruction of self and other.

But still the risen Lord stands with tears in eyes
Outstretched hand declaring hope, peace, love.
Men look at his pierced hands and bloody head and fear.

Margaret and Alan

23

The Old Church

The smell of damp licked around my nostrils
The damaged pews hid in the corner of my eyes
Mouldy carpets, scattered communion glasses,
A broken lectern stood limply to one side
A lifeless organ shouted "I've seen better days"
I stood motionless in empty despair and looked with tears
Even the rotted old flowers lay sapped of all their former beauty

All help to stir the air with a Soulless aroma of lost ness
Now joined by musty timeless songbooks of a former age.
A single Bible lay on the ground open but now unread.
Yet this was once a place filled with happy children
Singing praises to the living God.
A place where young couples came thrilled to tie the knot
A place so filled with hope that people dare not pass by
But were drawn in by sheer love.
The Organ was once proud to ring and sing with a
Wondrous sound that made the Angels sing for joy
The Lectern had stood in pride as the word of the living God
Rested in his arms
It had been a place of love and hope of faith but now
The only song that is sung is made by scampering mice
And the soft shuffle of beetles and bugs
I might have done something if only I'd spotted the trend.
But I have been so busy, money to make, games to play
Lord who is to blame? Who?

by Ashley Evans

24

If Only I had Known

It was a sunny day
And I was at sea
Then they said come and pay

Pay?
Yes there is a fee.

What fee? If I may say

You may say indeed sir.
Fee to ride in this ship

Free for me I do hope?

No Sir in to the pocket dip

No Sir I cannot cope!
The fee is too much I will not pay

OK sir the answer is clear.
GET OFF!

by Ashley Evans

25

Fear

The knife press against the small of my back
The deep voice said stand still
What are you doing I cried
Shut up or this knife will end you
I stood in fear, legs shaking
Why me? In fear and silence I stood
I stood for what seemed like hours
The voices uttered violence and anger
What will happen, I feel alone and very afraid.
I dare not think. I stood in petrified silence
Stood and stood, sweat poured from my head
When will it end and how will it end
It was dark now, bones throbbed in agony
Suddenly lights came on
From gloom came brilliant light
No knife in my back just quiet and stillness.
A voice rang out now kind and peaceful
Ten of you have been threatened
This my friends is what it is like
Around the world for so many
Just because they believe in Jesus
They show courage, great courage yet still many end up
    dead
Makes you think, so please leave here
Be grateful, be thoughtful and keep praying for
These dear people.

by Ashley Evans

26

Tremble

The dark sky issued fear and foreboding
Even the birds fluttered to hide,
cattle cower behind a rickety rocky wooden fence.
No sound, just the uncomfortable icy stillness
Cold fear gripped my heart, I stood and trembled
I looked, in the distance stood a figure
It seemed to move or was it my inner fear.
Was it my imagination? No, it did move!
It came closer, dark muslin covered the upper body
It moved reaching inside its hidden clothing
O no is it a gun? Will I get shot
He pulled out some kind of packet, opened it
He spoke. Have you a match Jack?
I'm dying for a fag.